Praise

"Addiction is not a subtle foe. It waits, always hungry, caring nothing for what we love. We lost a good friend when Jon passed and yet, here are his words, his heart still beating. This the disease couldn't take from us. Thank you Alycia for keeping him alive."

Jack Grisham, author director musician

"Vreeland's book is now a permanent part of my fabric, a very good part, and I can only reflect upon the author's reverence for Hemingway and Bukowski. Somewhere it was said that Jon Vreeland's inspiration drew upon the work of those two masters, but upon careful reflection, I believe it's the other way around."

Steven Kunes, TV Writer/Producer *Over My Dead Body*

"The world of Jon and Alycia Vreeland is not a pretty one, but it is real, vivid and memorable... By the end of *Laughing in Her Sleep*, you'll feel like you know the poet and the artist almost as well as you know yourself."

David Starkey, author of *Poor Ghost*

"Jon's poetry is like walking in the shadow of death; bringing insight into our pain. Alycia's art is the perfect balance to digest it."

Stacey Cameron

"With a kind of blunt honesty, Vreeland's poetic voice sounds much like his day-to-day voice—hard-edged, intense, raw, sometimes touching, and sometimes comic... Vreeland's work never ceases to embody life's complexities—the shock of truth and the bittersweetness of imagination."

Chella Courington, author of *Hearts Forged in Resistance*

About the Poet

Jon Vreeland was a self-proclaimed reincarnation of Hemingway.

A writer-poet-journalist-playwright, musician, born in Long Beach California and raised in Huntington Beach. Vreeland's writing appears in journals such as *Rebelle Society, East Fork, Sun and Sandstone, Plain Brown Wrapper, Painted Cave, Connoisseurs of Suffering; Poetry For The Journey of Meaning, Wealthy Lives Matter, Spill It: Vine Leaves Press.* Vreeland was president of the Writer's/Poet's Club at Santa Barbara City College. A journalist for *The Montecito Journal, The Santa Barbara News Press, The Santa Barbara Sentinel* and *Family Life Journal.* His major influences were Charles Bukowski, Ernest Hemingway, Jim Morrison, Darby Crash, God, his parents, and his two beautiful daughters, Mayzee and Scarlett. Vreeland was married to artist Alycia Vreeland.

jonvreeland.wordpress.com

About the Illustrator

Alycia Vreeland teaches art to little people near the American Riviera, writes about Baby Darlin' in her memoir, and plots revenge. She is soothed by taking one day at a time, twirling her hair, eating nachos, and feeling the Santa Barbara waves crashing on her toes.

Her art is featured in the documentaries, *The Cure* and *Guns, Bombs, and War: A Love Story* and online journals *Tuck Magazine, Rebelle Society, Painted Cave* and *The Montecito Journal.*

alyciavreeland.com

laughing in her sleep

a book of poetry

Alycia and Jon Vreeland

Laughing in Her Sleep

Print Edition
ISBN: 978-3-98832-079-7
Published by Vine Leaves Press 2024

Author and illustrator photos by Lara May

Cover design by Jessica Bell
Interior design by Amie McCracken

Dedicated to all
who continue to
struggle with addiction and
the children caught in the crossfire.
May you find hope and have a moment of clarity.

In Memory of
Jon Michael Vreeland
"my sugar"
R.I.P.

Jon Michael Vreeland
July 13, 1979-September 15, 2020

Jon Michael Vreeland, poet, author, journalist has died at the age of forty-one in Santa Barbara.

Born in Huntington Beach July 13, 1979 to two loving parents—Alyson Vreeland and Jon Vreeland.

He is also survived by his wife Alycia Vreeland; daughters Mayzee Vreeland, Scarlett Vreeland; stepson Preston Towers; and sister Christa Vreeland Bailey.

Jon is the author of *The Taste of Cigarettes: A Memoir of a Heroin Addict* and a former journalist.

Jon envisioned himself as a modern-day Hemingway with the influence of the unabashed vulgarity of Charles Bukowski. He wrote with such brazen honesty. He battled with drug addiction throughout his life and it was often a muse for his inspiration. He liked to shock the reader in the hope of scaring them straight as depicted in the graphic nature of his memoir.

He was very passionate about helping students find the truth in their voice through storytelling while working in the English department at Santa Barbara City College.

Hunter S. Thompson inspired his journalistic style. Alycia often had the opportunity to share in his love for writing and journalism, going on assignment as his Gonzo photographer.

Alycia met Jon through the love of his girls. She happened to be sneaking a peek over his shoulder at a church meeting, as he was admiring photographs of them on his phone. She commented on how beautiful they were. He turned around with a great big smile with such pride and joy and informed her they were his precious daughters.

His memory lives on for Alycia through his literature and their love of the countless creative adventures they shared together.

He is so missed by many.

"Death has eyes of ruby mirrors, skin of sapphire junk." J.V. Po

the taste of salt

Silence,
then crunching of gravel, under my black beat-up Chuck Taylors.
What are they looking at?
What do they see while locked in a casket?
Mahogany, black, white, or whatever color the mourners preferred.
Buried under six feet of earth soil.
A layer of green for the topping.
I wonder if their eyes ever adjust to the dark or are feasted on by critters residing amid the rotting corpse.

The wind's placid serenade breaks the silence.
I sojourn at the first row of bodies, who dream of slumber, which I am unconversant.
You, on hands and knees.
I struggle to read the inscription on the black marble gravestone, adorned with silver sparkles.
Its veneer, a seamless match for the prominent night sky.
Carmen Nieves Beloved Mother and Daughter 1902-1983
I could almost feel her gallant breath.
Her heart rattled, the precious diamonds placed on her smoldering chest.
Her dress of silk, scarlet, like her lips.
Another perfect match.
There is nothing like a stroll through the graveyard on a warm winter night.

It was so romantic, this romance with death.
My number one held my hand, as we trudged amongst the shores of Huntington Beach.

I am saddened to see less of my mistress lately, oppressed by paranoia and no help to my long-suffering insomnia.

I did not miss her although she had saved my life a number of times.
I was perfectly happy with the one that habitually steered me into the abyss.
Ordinarily, both of them would pirate blood from wherever possible tainted toxins so deleterious regifted to yours truly.
Then my eyes inadvertently shut
and on that day my number one and I made love where my mistress was nowhere to be found.
Who cares if my skin is stained
red
white
blue.
How patriotic death can be.
Pitch black and oh so cold, I was all alone, no God, no Devil, no light.
I walked interminably through a shade of black.
No recollection of where I was or how I got there.
I heard nothing.
I saw nobody.
My own skin, which was as pale as the crescent moon, I saw the night before and everything and everyone had vanished.
In a treacherous state of seclusion, something dreaded since the days of Krissy and Jack
and I wanted out.

I could hear my feet with every step that sounded hollow.
Is this it?
Am I in hell?
I tried to scream but nothing came out
and the only feeling I felt was the feeling of sinking lower into whatever unwaveringly waited under my
Chucks

plummeting slowly into a place I knew I would dread
and God was not the host,
sinking
drowning
slipping underneath the surface.

But the surface of what?
I didn't want to know.
It couldn't be a place of serenity.
I had met the Devil recently and he didn't seem to have the compassion of a conventional comrade just a smile so beautiful,
seductive, eyes sparkling like unblemished pearls,
stolen from somebody's soul.
So I thought of the Devil's eyes and their impeccable shine,
a light in the distance slowly gets larger, closer.
I wanted to smile but I realized the futility of a smile would only make me a liar.

The tears rolled down their faces as they hovered above, looking down an unwanted well, checking for snakes before descending through the Black Hole.
I could taste the salt in my mouth.
My brain worked overtime demanding to remember what had happened. Nothing came to mind,
more salt
more light
more voices
my eyes fluttered
someone squeezed my hand and kissed my cheek over and over.
Now my lips.
More salt but not my own.
I heard her speak while I looked around to see where I was
more salt
mine

hers
the taste was not of the sea
with no sigh of relief and no remorse, from me our night continued
and our so-called life stumbled on
holding hands in a dim and desolate place.

Day after day and night after night
I walked aimlessly with no purpose
no direction
possessing a broken spirit
a contemptuous soul
this was living death
purgatory
no Heaven
no Hell
just me and my synthetic lover
and occasional visits from my mistress.
The one dressed in white.

This deadly love triangle provided a surfeit of wickedness disguised as love.
I awaited my death but I was already dead—the joke was on them, they were beating a dead horse.
I trampled over thousands of
dead bodies.
In the Carpinteria cemetery.
It was a beautiful starlit night and oh, so beautiful.
It wasn't the thought of rotting
dead corpse, skeletons dressed for a masquerade ball in fancy dress, wearing jewels so enchanting, so precious, not the shadows that danced gracefully by the light of the moon, hand in hand, silhouettes eternally in love, but the letter and numbers gilded on their gravestones, a brief summary of their lives.
name

beloved mother
beloved daughter
son
father
birthday
the day given an opportunity to live.
Precious marble stones that paint a picture, manifesting the people that mourned their absence.
At least for a brief period of time before they danced into the afterlife, or Heaven as some would call it.
That was the beauty I saw people who lead lives with purpose
meaning and passion.
Today
my lover
my mistress
the triangle
are gone
vanished into thin air
but only from my eyes
sometimes they visit my dreams uninvited
longing for my kiss
my touch and my obsession
romancing me so maliciously
waiting for my return
an effort to furtively abolish my resurrection
offering an invitation to once again
dance with the dead.

I would rather walk through the dark night
holding God's hand
with a thousand well-dressed corpses
smiling at the silhouettes
who continue to dance to the beautiful music
so hypnotic

so real
they are not dead
they never died
their life has just begun
spirits and souls in another world
the better world God intends for us
the world where guardian angels hover over our shoulders
camouflaged by thin air and sometimes human flesh
protecting us from demons and the devil himself.
A world where death does not exist.

a walk to the store

... is a chance to observe the world
around you;
to see the parked and noiseless cars
hear the songs of the wild animals
smell the flowers in the gardens
admire the cloudless sunny sky
and the smiles of the people
the breasts of all beautiful women.

or:

you can watch the gurgling trucks
hear the endless barks of many dogs
the out of tune tweets from the bird on the wire;
you can smell the dog shit on the grass
watch the cloud that hovers above Montecito
snap a picture of an old lady's frown
and even notice the asshole of a sick and wandering feline.
It's really up to you ...

a coffee shop in Surf City

At a coffee shop in Surf City
familiar faces and sandy feet crawl in and out of the ringing door
looking for a cup of joe
someone to notice them typing on their fancy new Mac
trying to become the next heavyweight like
Bukowski
Ginsberg
William Burroughs
writing their masterpiece:
their Women
their Howl
their Junky
their ticket from Poverty.
I have known the lady behind the counter for many years.
Her name is Tree
and yes, she's a hippy
has found Jesus
mothers a boys
smiles at my girls
pours coffee for the people crawling through
hot, cold, small, large.
At a Coffee Shop in Surf City
people go in and out of the bathroom
living
dying
waiting for the rush to give them a reprieve

before they return to a world spinning faster than the coffee decides
with their shiny new Macs and cups of joe
as they peer through the glass of the ringing door
leaving the sand crusted on their tired feet.
another cup please
coming right up Mr. Vreeland
this one's on the house.

orange

I watched the Mexican and his hair in the
Plexiglass mirror.
It was breakfast,
we were standing in shades of color before the doors opened,
silence was all that was spoken of,
other than the faucet so the Mexican could style his hair.
I can't wait to see what is dying on the menu today and tonight.
Green eggs
a piece of brown wood that looks like Spam
red meth
sixty winds of stale and weary orange breath
or the furtively desired and hairless shadowy dead animal.
Nothing compares more righteously to the crowded solitary morning's essence
and if I were to die here my babies would have pearly teeth.
I never saw anybody's tongue or their eyes before breakfast.
It was barely 5 a.m., most wanted to return to their pilfered lies and metal divans,
while some are conversant with his habitat and this is all they dream of
and this dreadful color orange is something that is worn pompously
and the soft sink water they rub through their scalps washing the letters they picked
on their already tainted hairless heads.

the rich and the dead

Whitey was trudging over the
Newport Bridge
past the Rueben E. Lee
the Dunes, toward Fashion Island to park the yuppie cars
so they can spend more money
on more *things.*

My windshield cracked, the sun
shooting through its broken web—
its rays landing on my *still drunk from the night before face,*
pulling beads of toxic sweat down my cheeks, onto my
black jacket, my black pants and into my bleeding eyes.

I laugh with a cigarette dangling from my dried-up lips
as the sun continued to slap me in the face.

I could smell the aftermath
of the beer,
taste a hundred cigarettes,
from her snake bitten lips (her red lipstick smeared on her chin;
a whore with class).

I pulled into work suffocating
from a twenty-year demise
waved at the parking lot attendant, before he let me
through.

I parked a Rolls Royce,
a Bentley, a Benz, a BMW,
(I even kept them close by so they didn't have to wait for their car very long when they returned).

An hour later
I fetched the cars,
(whose wheels were worth more than my life), wishing the morning dew would sting my pallid face.
And for one lousy buck, and a year with no rain.

apartment A vs C

Students stay up all night long;
screaming
yelling
dancing
playing like young adults, enjoying their unwanted youth,
until the moon splits and the sun makes their shadowy eyes bleed.

In Apartment C
A young family is born;
screaming baby
tired mother
pissed off father from the long hours—
his colossal plumbing truck stands valiantly in the tenant parking
taking up two spaces
making the students park
somewhere else—I sit on my balcony and watch the endless feud with
my
beers,
smokes
bong and books.

I watched the young dad
drooling like a rabid wolf
headed to apartment A
a Louisville Slugger held tightly in his hands
eyes on the

luminous porchlight the students left shining vehemently
piercing the young father regretted life.

I watch the students party
like the children they are;
a revolving door of punks, surfers, even some hippies,
exploring life
each other
drugs
smiling and laughing in the night
sleeping while the sun burns violently.

(While the angry dad slash plumber, literally deals with everyone's grimy shit).

That night I watched a million pieces of glass strewn across the moon and sky.
The furious dad
showering
bathing himself in the shattered glass
from an innocent—
now murdered—porch light;
screaming like a monster
holding the bat overhead
a hand on each end
his silhouette dancing on the front wall tall like Lincoln
fangs like Darby Crash;
the unforgettable pearls of an angry plumber
a rueful-less dad.

The students did nothing.

the piano

The piano has sat in the corner
under the chandelier for years
with thousands of
drinks
pictures
candles
sitting on top of it, fading finish
and the light of
many suns and many more moons.

The piano sits in a
world of desolation
dying,
waiting for someone to touch and feel it like a man would a
woman (or vice versa of course).

An amiable form of foreplay
which only required a few notes
or a couple of cords.

The sustain is gone
the pedals are broken from
the movers when they broke it!
"a profession in itself ma'am!" he said, handing her a metal screw and a
bill through the roof.

Its keys are flat and sharp
six are broken in the
lower octaves
the strings are rusted
and the paint is waning
and soon
we will have to cremate the piano
like a conventional corpse
Send it off to heaven with the other dead instruments.
The other dead gods.

occupation

I needed a break
a reprieve
So I drove to the market
picked up two bottles of cheap wine
burgers (sold cheap).
I forgot the smokes
forgot the chocolate
but she wasn't mad
(I remembered the wine).

I needed a drink
writers
artists
musicians
have it bad.

Our souls are screaming on wax and dead trees
for people to
judge
gawk
criticize
envy.

Art is painful
stellar, artists are the same
verbatim.

(I poured the wine).

My eyes dragged down by rotten grapes
dripping from a dirty glass
the second full moon
powder blue
like her eyes.

Artists need rest
TV is a sure way to fall asleep.
(Nothing but garbage and empty soul)

40 on black

I used to swing a hammer
for an old man
He would bring his dog to the site
tied him up all day.
Poor mutt.

Just sitting in the sun
smiling at us
as we work in the sultry sun
up on the roof.

I could taste the beer
from the night before
the old man smelling the stale beer
and the dog is smiling.

He paid us on Fridays
Some of us came back Monday
asking for an advance.

"What happened to your cash?"
the old man asked.

"What do you think old man?
Forty on black got me again!"

The old man never scoffed,
never yelled,
swung his hammer
like the rest of us.
No booze
no whores
no drugs
no Jesus.

(Just a small pickup truck and us bastards
swinging our hammers)

Waiting for the next job
and the dog keeps smiling.

daddy declamation

All of us stood on the balcony as the smoke
crawled through the glass of the maternity ward seven pounds, two ounces on the eve of Halloween; a face stolen from God's secret stash that made everybody cry,
especially me. We celebrated with stolen cigars we claimed were from Cuba-friends.

The Dawning of the Queen. I watched you every day rolling crawling, ambling like a well-
oiled infant, a smile that could cause a ten-car pile-up, a celestial laugh that could rip the salt out of the toughest man's eyes, leaving him sobbing like a little girl.
The doctor cut you out of your crying mother—she herself,
just a child—holding my white knuckles now purple.
Listening to the group of medical junkies talk about LSD
and the Beatles and your silent scream still rings in my ears
you were wrapped in blood
and a tousle of your mother's innards
and nothing could have been more beautiful.

Bukowski

I met him in the county jail.
His honesty wasn't something I heard from anyone in a long time.
He was someone I believed.
Someone who had seen a thing or two. Scared people with his drunk-enness, his rancorous eyes,
his youthful punch (so he says).
He got me through those ninety days of almost sleepless nights
in the dorms with a hundred other men
farting
snoring
lying about their girlfriends,
(the ones they didn't have)
while he told the truth about the boils,
his twenty years of unwanted virginity,
his dreadful hangovers.

The inmates would ask me every single day:

"Whatcha readin' Jonny?
"Nothin', don't worry about it"

(I didn't introduce him to the other inmates, there were only a few of his books and I wanted them all to myself, plus I don't think many would understand his prose poetry and pain like me).

At 5 a.m., we would eat breakfast,
then return to our bunks until quiet time was over at 10 a.m.
This was the time I got to know him best
why he drank so much,
why he hated his father,
didn't like his mother,
why he wrote short stories about rape
and nobody got mad
or upset like they do when
I even say the four-letter word,
the one worse than the
Queen Mother of Dirty Words.

(Maybe those stories were unread? Or maybe
they fathom his pain as well?)

Maybe they have never heard of you either
Mr. Chinaski.

And after we are done playing pinochle, spades, working out, watching TV, watching or partaking in sometimes up to three fights a day, depending on the meals we were fed, or not fed at all, when there were no letters for me at mail call and the lights went out.

the walk

They bathe in unimaginable filth,
dripping salt from their rosy cheeks.
The creek is empty now and the red monster stealthy slumbers.
The man dreams of the sandy beach
and an aberrant glimpse of a shadowy graveyard
on the other side of town.

in the mornings

In the mornings there are
walls of flesh
walls of bone
waiting for me
like me shmoozing the lady
behind the glass.

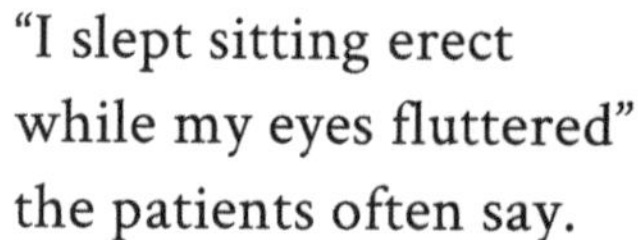

“I slept sitting erect
while my eyes fluttered”
the patients often say.

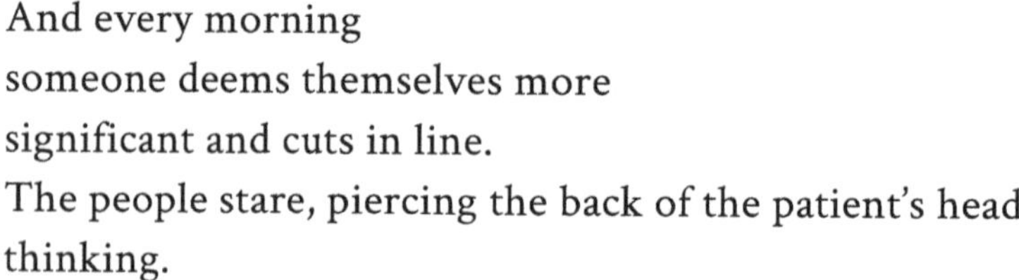

And every morning
someone deems themselves more
significant and cuts in line.
The people stare, piercing the back of the patient’s head
thinking.

“Make way for the King or Queen!”

(his inked up head
bulges with his remaining veins
his rope madness!)

When the door finally swings open, I walk the white hall with the many doors and two more women smiling behind two more panes of glass. “How are you today Jon?”

But the answers always sounds
the same and when I leave back to my car I tell them goodbye
(and never ever want to stay).

That very moon
I slept erect once again
and she was beside me, naked
laughing in her sleep.

Waiting ...
as the moon held high
matching her grin.

For the walls of flesh
walls of bone and the ladies waiting patiently behind the
three panes of glass.

diner by the bay

I was thinking about the night
the highway was empty
and we drove to the Diner by the Bay …

Only two little lights
were in my rearview mirror.
We drove in silence
smoked cigarettes
one at a time
one after another.

Until the box was left with little
brown crumbs.

"Why do you do heroin Jonny?"
"I don't, baby, heroin does me."

(She hid behind a cloud of blue smoke
as she picked at the dirt
under her nails
once painted black)

"Let's eat baby, there is a Diner right there
next to the bikers' bar and water tower."

"Do they have salad?"

"Of course, baby, whatever you want"

We rolled into the parking lot.
Two men were yelling
and screaming
showing the veins in their red foreheads
blood in their eyes,
so we sat by the jukebox and played Elvis.

"Listen to 'em sing, baby,
just listen"

"What is he singing about, Papa?"
"He's singing about you, baby,
you and your perilis cunt."

I got up and walked to *el baño*
(the man in the next stall heard
the flick of the Bic
and simmering boil as I
prepared the junk in my
not-so-silver spoon).

When I returned we ordered food
and drank beer and talked about it all.
Laughed about it too.

A procession of drunks
the smell of cigarettes
on my fingers and her lips

reminded us of a Vigilant and Avid God.

dancing with toads

My decorum frightened her.
My stories
written
lived
adorned.

A virtuoso and brother
disconsolately trudging
through cities that near
Emerald Maw.

Smirched and abounded in salt
I have heard her declamation
more
than
once.

“For he is spoiled and wants to steal
the one with sallow and twisted teeth!”

She even dreamed
of my deft intervals;
my many patrons;
my trifling dance with my fellow toads.

She wore an interminable grimace.
Insipidly
until the day I saw the moon
solely
in countless
vivid
dreams.

Where everything is
solemnized and the men
habitually dress in
not so
rueful grins.

So I finished the letter
and walked—
a smiled crawled upon her face
as the
not so prim were
waiting in an
immersed room;
a vastness of flesh,
marked by men
incessantly playing with
ignoble peerage
and
dirty needles.

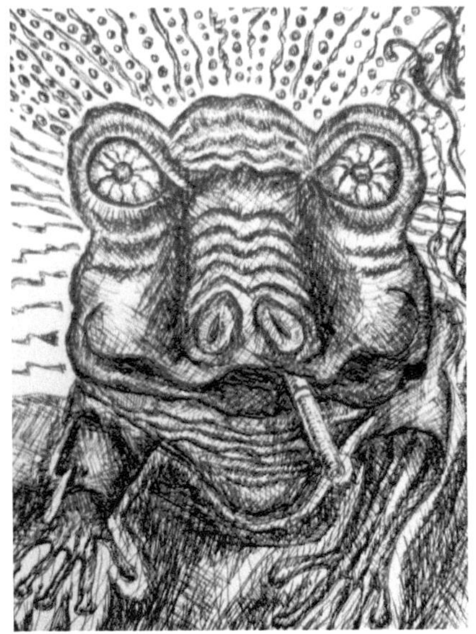

grandpa and the young Hispanic

She was mad.
It was Sunday and she was mad
so he drove his old pickup to the
store.

He bought:
chocolate—a whole pound
red wine—the cheap kind
ice cream—peanut butter and vanilla
and paid with a twenty.

But that was after
a young sly looking Hispanic
with a young sexy girl
brown hair
brown eyes
brown skin
(Waiting to be taken away from
the youngster,
into the arms of a
real man.)

Trudging through the parking lot,
they stopped at the brand-new
white Mercedes
stood at the trunk

slowly putting in their
two paper bags of groceries.

The man waited in his pickup
Johnny Cash
telling him a story about Jesus—
the story of His
murder.

He watched the young couple
climb into their brand
new car
(mommy and daddy's way
of saying
I love you)
His time was up.
There were five cars lined up behind.

The old pickup;
so the man walked to
the driver's side door of the
white Mercedes
ripped it open and saw
the young Hispanic's eyes jump
out of his shivering skull.

"Are you leaving?"
(The man almost yelled)

"yeah I'm leavin', I'm leaving!"

"Then get off your phone and do it!"
(He screamed in his face)

He slammed the door
The window cracked—a glass web was born.
They sped off
almost hitting two pedestrians on
their way out of the parking lot.

(He could see the fear in his eyes
hear the fear in her voice when she
screamed on the other side of the web
to go!) ...

... the man climbed into his old pickup
put the bag of groceries on
the passenger seat in place
of *her*
locked the bag in with
the seatbelt
so the wine bottle was safe.

When the man got
home he drank the wine
got a little
drunk and thought about the youngster,
the youngster who
will
probably
Not
forget that moment for a
long time
(the guy with rancorous eyes
screamed at him and his girl,
the guy listened to
Jesus Music
in his old pickup truck).

I know that is what they
must
be thinking,
Me and My Rancorous Eyes;

(but just like my grandpa always said)

“If you think I am bad now,
Imagine how I would be
if I didn’t believe in Jesus.”

child of God

They have been inside for years, trying to escape,

behind the red door

dozens of them smothered in black.

Soaking in a surfeit of poison,

the door remained locked.

Painted red.

They screamed for help;

How much longer can the demons hide?

Meth Monster,

children of the night,

strumming strings of madness,

tickling black and white, controlling them concisely,

living madly in disdain for so many years,

she covered them in words that came straight from the

depths of hell

with riveting savor.

A re-incarnated Etta James, but only for a while.

The door was still painted red.

Showing signs of black.

To be adorned by such demons can be overwhelming.

To be adored can be futile in the bitter end

(too many expectations).

Let the demons out to dance with the seraphs.

At last they will meet.

But first ... you must unlock the door.

Set them free.

Free the Monsters of Meth

Children of the Night that haunt you everyday

and night ...

no infamy

no ignominy

(Do not be afraid to be adored. You are a child of God).

up on the cliff

I live across the street from a graveyard
on a green hill but after work
I sit on a cliff and watch the ocean's
smooth glass
white caps
silhouettes of other islands.
There is a restaurant and a full bar
that sits down below
on the sand.
And it won't be too long until I leave this place
and land on my bare feet.

Outside the bar is a green truck and
it's always there.
And I'm always here
on the cliff above the sea,
not the cemetery on the green hill.
A cruise ship
parks by the pier and waits for the
passengers to get on and off,
talking about
E. coli, bad fish and the *Titanic.*

And there is a man.
The same man everyday asking for a cigarette
staring too long at my body and not my face.
It won't be long before I walk away
to bigger and better dreams, I am only around the

corner from my friend's
grandma's house who passed away
and left a house sitting in the sun
on the cliff with
nobody sleeping
eating
getting drunk
or fucking inside.

I live across the street from where
she is buried
rows of corpses and tombs
some names Elvira
and a crucifix on the top left
of the tombstone draped
with beads
and smaller cross swinging on the end
but after work I sit on the
cliff (not at grandma's house where she might creep inside)
smoking
cigarettes and watching the sea.

I can see sailboats
people on the beach
the bar and the islands
and it won't be long until I walk away from this place—
from the red roof and
green truck
cruise ships
the guy staring at my body—to bigger and better things
like living in a house with a woman's ghost
miles away from the green hill
with a cemetery mounted on top,
like a Scarlett Rose in the shadow of a
tall black hat topped with a
new Autumn Moon.

nightmares and good mornings

It was just after midnight when I woke up
dreaming all night
waking up every hour
pacing the house half awake
half nude
left the computer on as usual
I sat in front of a blue screen
shook the mouse until
an article about William Burroughs—
summing up his junk filled life—
turned up,
and all of his relapses
and outburst involving his gun and "queer bars"
I didn't know
he died still addicted to Junk
And holy shit
he was eighty-three when he died
that's old for a junky.

About 3 a.m. a taxi pulled up in our alley
procession of drunks arguing about
who was going to pay the driver
stumble out of the cab
and proceeded to announce their
nocturnal presence;
I was leaning on the screen door

face pressed against the mesh
staring at the commotion outside
I thanked God one more time ...

The hood popped we were on the side of the road when the white truck pulled up behind us with high beams stabbing our eyeballs with its white piercing light and a man got out of the truck, a man without a face, and told us to get in his truck
so we ran
our legs rubber, our shadows hastily fading ...

... I ran outside, ripping of my clothing one piece at a time
running desperately for the cool morning air
despite the sun climbing the blue sky
sweat descending down my brow
and into my eyes
I had to take a piss
so I blindly made my way to the bathroom
saying good morning to my naked wife on the way
holding my *girthy-schlong*
until it drained in the toilet
where a cigarette butt floated
in a lake of old orange piss.

decay and spring

We parked Whitey on Oceano.
Walked across the bridge to "the reading."
White chairs lined on the balcony
(like a wedding I attended when I smoked Salvia,
one of the places where the devil and I met)
half of them held asses of "poets and
writers" (at least that's what THEY called themselves).
Behind the stage
the east side of the city glowed
sirens howled
croonin' the night amid the abandoned
felines of Milpas Street.

The violins screamed
as she told a sad sad story of her
husband's sudden demise.
(it was the screaming that delayed my sleep,
saved it for later),
the other poet had edge and red glasses
resting on her nose as she read only
the nights' serenade,
no screaming violins.

We walked across the bridge
where Whitey waited—smoking cigs from
a blue box with a picture of an Indian on the front

smoking a peace pipe—
watching stars get closer
We walked uphill, her frail inked up finger
wrapped around my leather sleeve.

We opened Whitey,
climbed in, lit a joint, started the engine
made a left, made a right,
rolled past the blue house
with the rotting corpse,
the half-painted gate, white and gray,

(decay and spring crawled up our noses,
along with the salted windy sea).

We parked Whitey
listened to the clicks
the clacks.
finished our smokes.
went inside,
read Bukowski
crawled into bed
closed our eyes
an hour and a half later
woke up
opened the blue box with
the Indian on the front
smoking his pipe

right after we made quick,
Invincible Love.

church of grace

We walked past the cemetery across the street to the
white Painted Church
people in line holding numbers
empty bags
stolen shopping carts
waiting for them to be filled like a
pillow case on Halloween.

There is a garden and a man walking around
killing the veggies
carrots, zucchini, broccoli
the men smell like booze
and the women are pregnant
mothers of six seven eight young
kids running wild
holding expensive phones with cracks
drawing more eyes
from the meek that stand there
adoring the mountains and blue skies.

The guy in front
his head, turns at everyone in line
shakes his deprecating hair
rolling his eyes
and we laugh
and hope he wants to fight

(we know we never will)
And the man in the garden keeps
walking
stomping
killing
the
asparagus
tomatoes
mushrooms
and the kids still run through the concrete yard
waiting for, Momma and Pappy.
more bags of food
with more cracks in their phones.

I appraise an old lady of my assistance
next Saturday
a volunteer
she stared through her little metal frames
like I was crazy yet shrewd
(Like I wanted to submerge *myself* in the
mashed potatoes).

The long line of people slithering out the back door,
bags filled with food from *Supermarkets*
walk back to the streets with
the shadows' demise;
there is no school no church
no football no kids no family
no dope;
and no heart and no soul and no tears
from my baby's mother's eyes.

We walked past the cemetery across the street from the
White Painted Church

with bags of food and mirror-like phones
to our home and Whitey parked in front
leaking
a river of green under its radiant
ashen eyes.

the city crawling with vicious cats

The city is crawling with vicious cats
they hiss and prowl all morning and
all through the amiable night ...
I drove Whitey to McDonalds then to the
clinic this morning
where two women were outside screaming
with yellow eyes.

"It's my turn bitch!" "Fuck you bitch!"

I watched them circle each other
slowly
like a couple of animals
felines
showing fangs
ready to tear each other apart
by the time I parked the car
and walked to the front door of
the clinic
the two women were halfway down the street
still screaming
then quickly hidden by the
blazing sun.

After I drank the
clear medicine from the clear cup

I drove to the food bank
to *the church* where
there were two *different* women in the parking lot
screaming
yelling
dancing around each other like
Rizzo and her Pink Ladies
ready to rip each other's hair out then sell it on eBay
(I couldn't hear what the fight was about
but the language was practically the same)

"Fuck you bitch!" "You whore!"

One was holding a tray of cupcakes
yelling with a
green and purple tongue.
She was
much older
much shorter
much meaner
had more tattoos than me
the other girl twice her size,
a little scared
and holding a giant ham
(I could tell she wanted to heave at the
short firecracker
or jam it right up her ass
and laugh in her face;
or is that what I wanted to see?)

The girls were getting louder
taking the ham and cupcakes with them
they trudged through the lot
and walked into the sun

I stood in line with the rest of them
wondering why all the
women were fighting and acting vicious toward
one another and not *us* today?
who cares
just enjoy it while it lasts, I thought
enjoy it while it lasts.

his dick has a shadow

It was Thanksgiving and the man was
lying on the bus stop with turkeys and big plates
of food the people kept bringing him.
It was ridiculous.
What is he even going to do with a turkey
let alone eight?
(If I were the guy on the bench I would ask the
people that too.)

"Look, you see all this food
all these turkeys?
What the fuck am I supposed to do with even one?
You really are making more work for me when all
I want to sit out here staring at the sun."

But the people aren't doing it for the
King of the Bus Stop
they are doing it for themselves
so they can bring it
up in casual conversation

"What did you do today, Dick?"

"Oh you know just got the kids ready,
washed the car, took a turkey to that guy on
the Bus Stop."

"Oh really? You are such a good soul, Dick."

When I drove by later
the man was gone
and all the food was left behind
being ripped apart by
raccoons and opossums
an orgy of rabies and sharp teeth
(nobody was there to clean up the mess
I have never seen such disorder.)

"But at least the man knows he is loved."

"Yes, I'm sure he's been staring at the sun
praying for a rabid animal to devour
his Thanksgiving."

I met a relative of Edgar Allen Poe

I met a relative of Edgar Allen Poe
standing on my path
leaning on my tree

smoking weed and cigarettes
he kindly offered me both
I accepted.

He didn't look like Ed;
his hair was blond
he wasn't wearing black
he wasn't drunk
or fighting with other writers
or wallowing over a girl
or planning a murder.

Yet he claims their blood is the same
(third cousin according to his dad's research).

"I like Poe, he's a crazy romantic Gothic too."
"He's my relative."
"I know you told me."
"Smoke?"
"Yes."

The longer I stayed
the more the stranger talked of Ed,
(but I don't know if I believe him).

He plays music
but is not a writer or a poet
and the only thing he writes is
non-rhyming jingles
and he has a white pocket full of cash.

(I read him a poem; he said nothing at its end
just lit another fire
while staring in the trees.)

I met a relative of Edgar Allen Poe,
I know this because
the very next day I saw the man
sitting against my tree
mumbling and gazing
to his utter death.

view from 777

Across the street from the taco place
with music
young waitresses wearing
practically nothing and smiling extra big
so you will leave
them more than a 20% tip—
Is a motel with twenty-five
rooms and even more windows and on the third story
you can see
Catalina Island and the emerald sea
and the tops of palms
and roofs of housetops in Surfside
and it invokes my boss
and the other carpenters that built with us for years
And next door is a sushi place
It's the kind of
place that makes me want to
drink before I go inside because of all the
douchebags
that work behind the bar
and even in the back with the
decapitated fish
and hidden bottle of hot sake
Sam's Seafood
is next to
the sushi place and they have live music

blues and jazz
An
old black piano sits in the corner,
waiting for me to play a song that will
be forgotten before the

Triple 7
3rd Floor

the bums on the grassy knoll are sleeping in the graveyard

When I was in college I spent a lot of time
sitting under a giant tree—
its parts and branches tangled—
smoking cigarettes
reading literature
Bukowski Hemingway Faulkner
scribbling in this red book
meeting people every day;
students going to
class
people passing through
with a 40 oz. of Bud and a joint
The ones who stop to talk are usually
lonely
good
spirits
they comment on the trash thrown
down in the ditch next to my tangled
throne
bottles, cans and boxes of
beer wine whiskey vodka
most of the students have accents
German Russian Swedish Mexican
some don't speak

English at all
most ask for a cigarette and
seventy-five percent land the deal
with me
the others are told
No with no explanation whatsoever
This one guy
kept pushing me and wouldn't let up

"c'mon 'bro' I'll give you a quarter"

"a quarter? Well gee thanks Aunt Bee
no foolin' a whole quarter?"

"Okay okay a dollar then,
I'll give you a dollar for one lousy cigarette"

"I got better idea junior
why don't you fuck off before
I throw you down into the graveyard of booze"

(I watched his feet go faster and faster
as he practically ran away)

When I was in college I also spent time
on the grassy knoll
on the other side of the campus
It looked over the part of the
Pacific

the Garvin Theatre
and another one trying to close the deal
with me (this one in more ways than one)

“Look man I am not a fucking convenience store.
Do you even go to this school?”

“geez what is your problem bro”

“I ain’t your brother, my mother is a saint” I told him
as I walked away

But the rest, the rest are good
spirits,
usually making
love to their desolate drunken souls
carrying actual books
Shakespeare
Faulkner
Dunbar
Freud
learning more languages to create
more accents
not even alcoholics or whores yet
babies with baby beer fat
and bank accounts.

There was one more sitting under the
confusion of the tree.
He asked for a smoke

“Sir sir may I have a grit?”
“Sir? Grit?”

And with no explanation whatsoever
... down he went
... down he went
... down he went

bad actress small symphony

It was just past 10.
She went to sleep.
I stayed awake trying to write
watching the inaudible TV
commercials about beer
steaks lobster and beer
sitcoms that don't deserve volume
sitcoms that kill brain cells like
huffing gas from a Coke or Pepsi can.
I play a record
instead
of the TV getting to say anything
at all
(The piano and violins and
cellos and harps make
more sense anyways
have more to say.)

(I light a cigarette
it's a Camel-filtered
not a *chode.*)

And the two women on TV
are bad actresses
possibly uneducated as well.
I checked out four books today

so I can read and not have to listen
to the TV but only
watch the bad actresses.
I play Beethoven or Mozart or Brahms
let them narrate the silence
(hoping in the morning she is still here).
It's a quarter till midnight.

The music is still taking over the
silent screen
my cigarette is still burnin'
and the smoke stays away from my eyes.

80 breasts, 5 cocks, 11 testicles? (for a secretive artist)

I am writer, a poet, I write down feelings on paper
in a red book with a magnet
so it stays shut and others can't see.
I carry a black pen in case I get an idea or
see something
or yet evoke something.

Yeah I write about women and
their discrepancies.
How they force me to internally vacate.

(Sometimes I cry when I get mad or frustrated
or confused when I lose my keys and I'm late—
but only sometimes not often.)

So I write a poem or a story—
involving something or someone that is
sad and possibly dead—
read it to her while we drink
two bottles of wine and smoke two or three
laughing bones.
If she doesn't like it I usually threaten
to slap or murder her.

(she laughs when I announce my alleged vileness)

And I have taken a yoga class from the
world's biggest bitch—
she had short hair and a really fat ass—
with mostly women in the class.
80 breast and maybe 5 cocks,
and 11 testicles?

I also play piano and sometimes wear mascara
war paint,
carve ink in my skin
a girl might stretch draw or paint

I read poetry too from men and women
some alive
some dead.

And I bet I can kick your ass all over
this place until you cry like a baby.

(I've been called loser and faggot one too many times)

bus and the sway

I didn't see what happened when the city bus
rolled past on the street,
just the smeared faces of the passengers.
Inside—someone had written: KILL THEM ALL!
on the city bus window with green and red
paint.

"He walked home after work and sharpened a
dull piece of metal loaded his gun shoved it in
her mouth until it exploded, she gagged twice.
She was dangling from her window naked and
screaming soaking wet water dripping from
head to feet hiding tears sweat, and his cum
from anyone who was there, and then the cops
showed up in loud cars."

Another bus came, faces dragging until
the colors smeared. Again. Until nothing but a
pendulous corpse
turning red from the sun
appeared
swinging from the neighboring tree
of the bus stop.

(The tree with the tree house and all those kids
who climb up and down like kids.)

The crowd watched her inert sway. Another
bus came, it was empty no tracers no heads
I could see her feet through the bus—no
passengers this time—through
both windows dangling from the sky.
Pointed at the dirt.
When the bus drove off
The coed had grown into a mob.
(Not an angry mob; a pleased, un-saddened mob.)

The silence evolved to chatter
Nobody knew her name.
The swinging corps with the long brown hair
hiding her unknown face.

"She was a stranger no worth crying over, plus
she'd done it to herself," a woman said.

She swung into the night as the mob remained.
A pastel moon climbed the night sky.

I didn't see what happened I only heard
The city bus rolled away and there she was,
swinging from the tree by her neck,
I really don't know what she was swinging.
But she sure is beautiful
(*I think I will wait until they all leave, and all
go to bed.)*

death of a muse

She had always spoke of death and it's
sheer grandeur.
At parties and balls for the governor
or perhaps a masquerade held at midnight
for the town's finest, in the town
cathedral,
driven in the town hearse painted white,
all wrapped in dead animals
stolen jewels on their mistress' arms.

She was an individual and quite
noticeable
and droll.
Smoked Benson and Hedges
held by a long piece of plastic,
held between her teeth,
Her tongue strained
as her lips told
stories of the women and their men
(and even their children).

But her tongue stretched too far,
slid in and out of her mouth
manifesting her exact sentiments of her peers.
Her facade smelled
like a woman,

and her tongue slid farther
until the cold ocean crawled upon
her black and vagrant toes.
Her skin began to crack red cracks
amid her blue furrows
while the town simply leaped over her
bloated flesh.
Urine and feces dripped down her bloated leg
onto her black and blue stumps
and dried a pasty brown.

(The copper resting on her dingy rags
desisted her former foes of any more
slander. She had always spoken about death
and its utter splendor, but it had been twenty
long years since she was
ostracized
from a world of sham elegance,
a world that would end her.)

Now face down
with her lids peeled to her head
A man—
who had furtively
watched her
invidious
scoff for years and years, from his
sixth story Veranda, who watched her go
from riches to rags—
painted the woman
covered in dirt piss and shit
lying in the barren gutter,
drowning in the town's *exquisite* water.

A demystifying demise.

a poem for my wife <3<3<3

Her Morning Glory
It is when black skies fade to violet
I see her hunched over
her wooden table.
Smoke slivering through her fingers,
fondling the kitchen light that spot lights and
illuminates her newest piece.
Lips like Warhol sewn with rusted safety pins
you stole from my jacket.
And in the morning when I hear our coffee
maker
on its last leg, brewing your morning fix,
I creep past
looking over your shoulder while Iggy Pop
sings in your ear and Marilyn dances on
pinstripes,
wondering if this will be the last one that
grants us the privilege to sleep in till noon,
swim naked in our pool,
and nobody sees me walking in the rain
to wait for the bus that is already gone.

drunk at midnight

The radio is loud,
the neighbors are pissed,
the cat is confused,
the door left open,
the cold viciously ignored,
insurmountable cigarettes burn
and
ashtrays overflow,
phones
beep,
ring,
vibrate,
sing,
(temporary lovers looking for their
occasional freebie)
the very audible television
plays infomercials
while some noses run
and most junkies sleep
while our Mothers worry;
Rocky Horror Picture Show plays,
the radio gets turned down.

mean versus cruel

I can be mean, but I can also be cruel.
Mean doesn't take much
just a simple "fuck you"
or a cold-ass shoulder will work
but cruelty takes performance
and it lives inside and drinks from
our veins
a fiend who wears the same shade skin as yours
palish-ugly
smirks with another set of lips.
I can be mean sure
but in order to achieve real-life cruelty
you must first rip out your very own
heart, toss in the goddamn stew or the
trash
and let the squirmy maggots breed.
That's right, men your very own heart
rip it out.
Then a woman's quickly after
and repeat that process for far too long
we don't need witchy flowers
or barrels of laughing suds
or candy from sixteen strangers
we don't need to touch a strand of our
unwashed hair
but in order to achieve real-life cruelty

you must first rip out your very own heart
toss it in the goddamn stew or the
trash
and let the squirmy maggots breed
that's right men your very own heart
rip it out
then a woman quickly after
and repeat the process for far too long
we don't need witchy flowers
or barrels of laughing suds
or candy from sixteen strangers,
we don't need to touch a strand of our unwashed
hair to brutally abuse the other
just use every name in the book and crush their soul;
but men make sure you scowl at her
like a wolf, believe me
they scare when we show our teeth
just paint their pretty dress scarlet
with their inside and your own
and then wave to the giant roaches
as they all creep in from the rain.

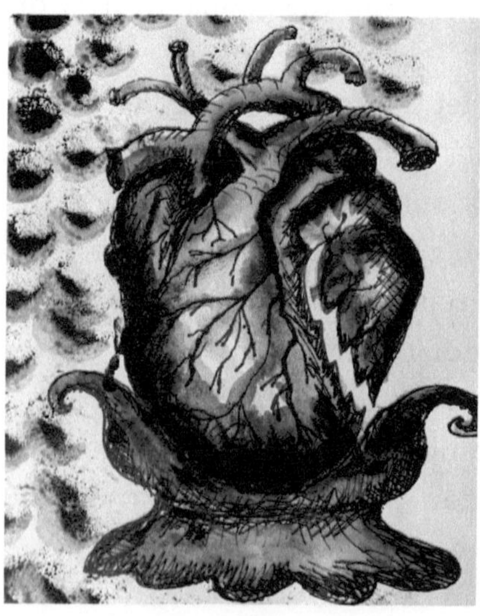

for the bums without collars

I was nineteen and broke
despite having a decent
job with UPS.

At dinner time and rush hour
I drove through the crowded hills of Laguna.

I drove my little red
Toyota pickup truck
to a giant warehouse
with
screaming lowlifes, alcoholics and drug
addicts—
America's finest assholes
with unrepairable teeth—

I loaded UPS delivery trucks
but I wanted to
climb the ladder,
maybe drive a big brown
beast that roars through the neighborhoods
and dines
with
Mrs. Robinson
and sail
on my forty-foot boat.

I worked that job
for close to a year; I wanted to support
my little family
and prove
I wasn't
a bum without a collar.

Eventually I quit that UPS.
I crawled backward
like a drunken crab,
fell smack
on my bony ass,
emotionally and financially.

now it's twenty years later
and I am a goddamn writer.

so,
financially at least,
things are worse than ever …

down the hatch

I hopped on my skateboard to get smokes
from the 7-11 around the corner.
It was a warm summer night and the moon was full
I only had ten dollars
so my girlfriend knew there would be at least
four dollars change.

"Camel filters please."

"Five-fifty."

I gave the Navajo ten.

"Four-fifty is your change."

On my skate back to our dirty apartment,
I see Bill.
He is walking his dog and leaves the
dog shit on the Asian ladies' lawn,
I always see the Asian lady walking down her driveway
to get the paper.
I always get a glimpse of her little
itty-bitty titties when she bends over to get the paper.

"Hey Billy what's up?"
"Just walking the mutt. Hey I've got some

Xanax if you want to buy any."

"Dude I have four bucks on me will you sell me one?"

"Sure man here you go,"
he says handing me the two-milligram pill.

Down the hatch it went.

I walked inside and my girlfriend had her feet up, painting her toes.

"Hey honey, did you get the smokes?"

"Yeah, here babe," I said, handing her a Camel.

"Change?"

"Oh I gave it to a bum."

"That was all of our money dipshit."

I never told her or anyone what I really did with the measly four dollars.

the cough the rain the cashier

The 101 was mobbed with
miles of rolling metal
with the drivers sitting in the wrong seat
the radio never satisfies us
just the flying monkeys
the pink ones
and the spell of
King Congo Powers
and his white guitar.

We forgot to stop for smokes and wine
so I jumped in the Ford and drove and
it was raining
the gas tank was empty and ol' Whitey
started to cough and whine
sounding like a former lover
All of them.

A pack of Camels.

I gave the cashier a ten
then handed me a pack of
Pall Mall.

These aren't Camels! I told the man
these are names after my papa

Paul
who they killed
and I am almost certain
they murdered my other
grandpa as well.

When he gave me the right pack
he had the balls to ask me for $6.85
so I told him to throw in a $3.00 Lottery ticket
Black Out Bingo
so I can feed ol' Whitey and
get my early morning fix
when he offered me the remaining silver.
I declined
and walked away scratching my skin
with my fingers crossed.

I won another ticket so I drove back to
the market.

(It was raining and the trees were meandering
and reaching for the ground)
and I saw my two pieces of silver
resting in the penny tray.

What an honest and noble cashier
I thought
then I handed him the winner
and asked for another ticket
and
walked back to ol' Whitey
and listened to her
cough
hack

and vomit like a smoker all the way home
where *she* waited for me.

“The man at the store was a good soul”
I told *her*
“left the silver in the copper tray
and didn’t put
it in his pocket
next to his balls!
next to his taint!”

“Which Store?”

“The same one we always go to, where do you think?”

“Yes, I know who he is and he raped me years back and
didn’t even like it or tell me that he loved me”

I crawled back to ol’ Whitey
Back to the rain
and Whitey’s
evolving hack

and won another ticket.

a bird's behind

I saw her running on the sand
her cheeks swung
side to side
up and down.

There were no boundaries
for the thing
and it was covered

with purple shorts that
barely fit the thing
It went straight up
and then straight down.

My eyeballs shadowed
the thing like a peeping tom
in hunt for his or her
(most likely his right?)
Prey
Victim
Lover

Did you see the last time!?
Straight up toward the sky!
Then right down where it belongs!
Twisting toward the dirt
like a sad old man.

I can't tell you what it looks like.
It keeps bouncing everywhere
with such radiance
such brilliance.

It's getting farther
I push the four wheels
faster on my board

all four of them
rolling toward her big behind.

Her giant ass!

Look at it fly up and down
like a dying bird
waiting for the sun to leave
so the moon can hide that thing.

Hide that thing as it keeps bouncing.

Bouncing in the half moonlight.

the bar

She smiled at me when I sat down
what a tangible woman
the type you find in a dream.

She sat at the bar
sipping her drink
ignoring everyone in the room.

She was much too beautiful for them;
Sloths
reeking of gin and cheap cigars
and the bottle with the old sailor ship
Business men who had told their wives.

“Baby I’m working. Got a real mess down here.
Right now we are fucked it’s gonna be a while.”

Yes, it was one of those days!!

But it was Tuesday
and nobody felt like working today
Working to remain in debt.

(Your phone will still scream
at 6 a.m.!! Leeches to suck you dry!!)

They were there to forget their lives
wives
kids
work
God etc.
But only for a while

I ordered another drink
and went to the bathroom to fix
when I returned to the bar her smile had vanished.

(vanished when she looked at me)

She glanced down my left arm
then walked out leaving her glass half full
and a cigarette burning.

mornings in the night

The middle of the night is early morning
shadows climb the neighbor's wall
she gets naked and grabs it.

The quiet night listens to her
moan and laugh like a witch trying not
to scream through the thin walls
of the *strangers* next door.

I sit alone and watch them crawl
while she sleeps
listen to the night and
her dreams.

(waiting for the sky to turn junkie blue)

While the crows begin to chatter
she boils a pot of coffee
and a pot of tea

and brushes her hair staring naked
in the mirror
on the back of the bathroom door.

While I wait for the whistling pot on the
burning stove

I eat
take vitamins
my medicine.

My eyes start to close
then we drive to work;
on the way I smoke three cigarettes
then walk up hundreds of steps
followed by total strangers.

Nobody says a word.

red car

I awoke with my head in my lap
like I was trying to
suck myself off.
A man was leaning on a red car
a cloud of smoke
wrapped around his hairless
head.
I could see him through
the screen door—but pretended
not to—watching the girl next door
when I shut my eyes.

I could still hear
Nico
singing like a foreign
angel
not thinking about the red car.
The man surrounded by
remains
of his bummed cigarette.

It was minutes
(or was it hours?)
I held my lids shut
my eyelashes twisted
tangled

barbwire
blocking my vision
making my left eye bleed water
when they untangle.

There he stood
his face pressed against the
dirty mesh,
one eye open,
“Good Evening” he said then
laughed a scratchy laugh,
walked back
to the red car and the
smoke followed.
He leaned on the door
and my head was in my lap.

$8.00 … and some change

We were driving his old beat up
Mazda hatchback;
between the four of us we had
started the night with
$32.00
Camel filtered—one pack
three warrants for our arrest and undoubtedly
an STD or two,
stalking its next victim

She gave the money
to a tall white boy
on the Costa Mesa Hill
for some
black tar
and two used syringes.

(It is hard to fret about something like
HIV
or Hepatitis
when your skin feels like tin foil
sweating under the blanket with chills
drenched in cold brown sweat.)

We hadn't noticed his skin
how it was

hastily changing color
as he sat in the passenger seat
of his own car.

We were enjoying our
absence from the world.

from God Himself

We headed northbound on Beach Boulevard
In the back seat we kissed,
ignorant to everything around us
while the twenty-five-year-old art student
was slipping away.

To a place that can only
be reached when He sends for you
even when your relationship has disintegrated
and there has been very little contact or none at all.

(Nobody wishes for a slow and
painful death
when it can be done in five minutes
slumbering
in the deepest most painless coma
your subconscious
has been yearning for because
you discovered the hastiest way of
killing the pain
and creating
an unspeakable amount, Simultaneously.)

On that dreadful night
not even twenty minutes after our money

was spent
the driver—
my good friend Dave—
started slapping the student in the face.

He barreled through a red light going
fifty miles per hour.

(A form of CPR that only people like *us*
were familiar with. It often worked.)

I screamed at Dave telling him to,
"Drive to the hospital!!
GO GO GO!!!
I took over the responsibility of trying
to bring him back
so he could have another chance at life.
I grabbed him by the chin and the top of his head—
sandy blond hair—
tilted his head into the backseat; the car
screamed up Beach Boulevard
to the nearest hospital.

My red stained lips to his.
I blow as much air into his lungs as
my body would allow.

She pounds vigorously on his
chest.

We arrived at the hospital.
Dave ran inside screaming
for help as we continued to
blow air in his lungs and
slap him to try and wake him up.

To save his contemptuous life.

Five minutes later a female nurse
walks slowly
through the automatic door
staring with a look of indifference
thinking:

Not another Junkie! Not another one!!

He died in my arms that night, under
a starless sky
and a coveted moon
tears of
anguish remorse envy
sliding down my empty pallid-face.

some days
march 20, 2020

I am unstoppable:
a story or a poem comes
with the greatest
of ease.
I make legends
like
Kerouac
Ginsberg
Sylvia Plath
look foolish,
illiterate,
unworthy
of my
presence;

their words become pointless
and the second I open
my faithful machine,
I turn simple walks to
the store
into a smidge of my wanted existence,
(and I laugh at those
who
try
so very hard to impress,

when all I did was take
the barking dogs
the honking horns
the hurling trucks
the howling of sirens
and then mold them into
something
novel and chic ...)

then, there are the other days ... the majority
of my dreams.

Days when I feel like a fraud,
someone who,
every once in a while,
gets lucky.
someone who doesn't deserve
to lick
the
dog shit
off a poet's least favorite
shoes.

don't call me a junkie

You may remember this man
waltzing the boulevard with one shoe
and shit-stained pants
and unholy eyes;
he watched the
common people zip by in cars they couldn't
afford,
with people they barely love.

Yes, you may remember this man;

he entered countless rehabs and
sober livings with the
souls who left their shoes in the gutter,
where they slept for
years and years, bathing with the rats
and the possums,
while their family lied to Grandma on Christmas:
"oh he's working somewhere
far away; we don't know when
he'll be back."
and the kids are told:
"daddy's sick right now
and we don't know when he'll be better."

You may remember this man,
he asked you for some change and you
gave that filthy hype a dollar to keep your
morals in tack.
And this man who waltzed the boulevard
with one beat-up shoe and shit-stained
pants
is now a "writer"

on a mission from
the gods
(who he never really knew, not until he found
his other shoe and changed his clothes
and his adamance about erasing labels of the finest cliches)

"don't call me a junkie!" he says.

January 10, 2020

David Foster Wallace was nuts
Hemingway depressed
Bukowski drunk
London loved the sea
Faulkner ambiguous
Bierce disappeared
Vidal the first literary goddess
Steinbeck a prophet
Poe the poster child of death
Hunter S. Thompson dropped acid
Trumbo was a black-listed "commie"
Burroughs an eighty-three-year-old junkie
under careful maintenance
and Oscar Wilde was a "fag"
Plath another goddess
Sexton a victim of love
Fante the greatest unknown
Elliot the largest asshole
Hubert Selby Jr. died for fifty years
and I'm on my way
to the most beautiful darkness
the world has ever known …

5 a.m.
September 27, 2018

I can smell the
coffee,
hear the birds chatter,
the
felines
fuck,
the sky melts
between
the dirty
white blinds
and
little sheaths of
light
lick the tops of
overpriced
shitholes,
(purchased
with
a brave co-signer)
and her snoring is melodic.
I sit and drink my dark roast
in front of an open window,
I light a Camel,
the felines sing

like gremlins,
songs before they
murder their young.

So I pour another cup
and
listen to the morning
scream.

off to find the dawn

My landlord knocks
I tell him to come in
and he does;
he tells me
my rent is past due
and that I gotta go.

I look at the piano,
wave goodbye to the
organ—a gift of blood
and lots of flowers.

I wave goodbye to the
paintings
as they laugh me into
submission.

I grab a single bag.
I fill it with clothes,
my favorite books:
poems by
Rimbaud
Bukowski
Carrol
and light a smoke
then walk into the rain,
just me and
myself.

just for her

We live in a one bedroom
manor in
Santa Barbara
—no howling flutes or
squealing trumpets,
just the sound of
an old piano.
I play just for her.

Henry the VIII

I met her on a Tuesday,
we drove,
along the shores of Montecito,
the artist with long
black hair
and pale blue eyes ...
we drove into the desert,
up a two lane highway
with King Henry the VIII,
and swam where immortals
drown in the harbor of felines.
#soulmates

my sweet deprivation

Without Her I am angry deprived of food
and many other things.
It's not a woman's job to feed me
they just do
and it started with my mother
"joge, eat your peas" then with
my various others:
"babe, eat something, you look like
an anorexic girl."
but without Her, I
can only sleep,
dreamless and cold.
I am weak ...

naked serenity

There's something insane about a lady in black clothing,
funeral attire mended with particular fashion, teeth
like a cat on the sweetest nod, perfection that shines on.

There's something inane about a disease with long buzzing
legs, while I rock like a broken chair made of
my shattered heart.

I'm a stranger inside unlit trailers, looking down the
barrel of a .45 that misfires at the touch of a Redneck's
decree.

As the moon crawls through the few stars of this cherubic
city, she's all I think about: I know a fairy tale
when I dream one, and she's the one that pets the serpent
with grungy hands, kisses my lips with the tongue
of naked serenity.

I hope we never fall in love again;

expectations of a lost puppy without any fur.

dear Buk

To be famous or to die a terrible death, a trip to the store
for eggs and beer may turn tumultuous;
the paparazzi with kaleidoscope lenses—souls with
tourniquets tied to their tiny sacs—will hogtie your outing
without a doubt.
You made a living talking shit on the elite, then made
friends with Sean Penn?
Drove a BMW?
Either way, old Buk,
I know life isn't easy, so I forgive you, but fame makes
death a lovely place, old Buk, a soliloquy I hope I never
endure.
You were wrong, you crusty poet:
FAME is a "dog from hell"; and LOVE is a flower without
bees
birds without wings.

a wild boy on a streetcar

Southern California is
ablaze on the first day of the
summer. The smoke billows
and paints the Orange
County sky a sad portending
gray with

no stars
no clouds

just smoke and the death that
hovers in the sky, the moon
red like the skin of a red—
Scarlett Rose. So I watch
Brando scream mumble rage
and rumble in Black and White

On the Waterfront

A Streetcar Named Desire

The Wild Ones

And I think to myself, while
my cigarette burns a gray
tornado of delicious smoke,

I want to be like Stanley
Kowalski, that crazy Pollock
the girls fear and make cute
fun of (Stella Blanche and Doris);
I want to eat greasy
chicken like a pig then
throw my plate against the
wall and scream in people's
faces, flip over card tables
and knock out three of my
friends after they stick me in
the shower.

sex and Salvador

Saturday ...
We walked on the sand
with one
pair of shoes
and two cans of warm beer.
The ocean stench
was familiar.
It smelled like the bottom
of the bag;
$4.68 from the best burger spot in town
and a free
shooting
gallery across the street
hidden
from the sun.

Impervious to
my dirty black jeans and
the luster of my
yellow teeth
she rolled up her outer sleeve
and uncloistered
her pallid stems
and Dali's
seven naked women form
a skull
someone had carved in her thigh.

I stabbed her in her left
septic arm
before she stabbed mine.
The third stabbing
was between her stems
above the women that starred
from spectral eyes
teeth made of toes.

Their feminine flesh.
Then two cherry tornadoes
and one
orgasm on this salted Saturday …
or was it Sunday?

We celebrated with two more
warm cans
and one
luminous moon.

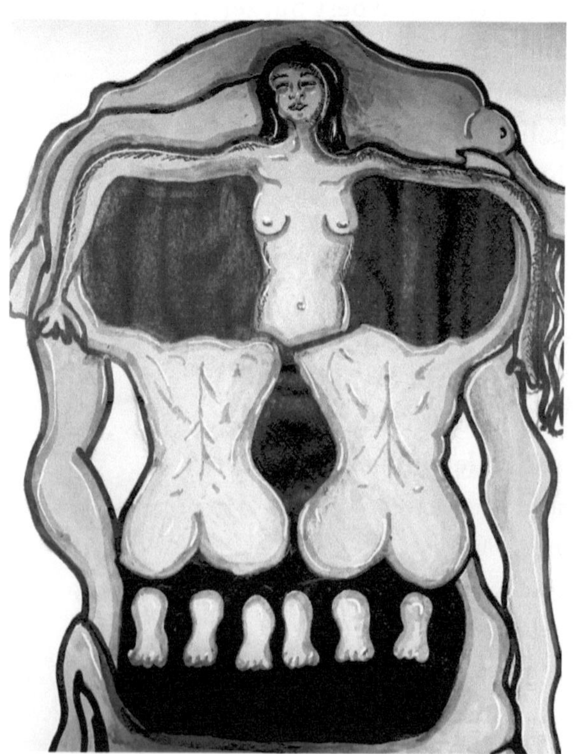

a rescue named Cindy

I already miss her.
Her blonde and brown hair,
her big green eyes.
She gave me a hug and kiss
every time I walked through the door.
She loved me when I was happy, when
I was sad: and when the demons were
inside me
she kissed my face, rested her head on
my lap and always told me it was ok.
She never scoffed.
Always grinned.
I already miss her terribly, but
I am glad she is not in pain,
(I am trying really hard not to be selfish,
but it's hard.)

the toothless old hag

Under the pier her diminutive place
her place of utter despondency.
Always prompted the thought of
his sullen face
rotting inside his white casket.

The Toothless Old Hag was old and gray,
Wore pearl around her old
flabby skin.
Her black hat draped amid her wily eyes
as she stared into the blistering sun.

She sat on the boardwalk talking to
strangers on her old wooden bench;
all day and night reading pose and poetry;
Bukowski
Tolstoy
Poe
Hemingway
(Ambrose was her desire.
His allusions to malevolence
made her drip)

She sang loudly! A melancholic hollow voice
that cracked like butter!
(like the lines in her face)

Only fools who have hit their heads fall in love,
only fools from down below and up above!!!

And when the blistering sun waned
she danced
under clear red skies
with her old saggy cheeks and the Toothless' Hags
shadow too.
Her big black hat is still covering her wily eyes.

(Because God was nowhere to be found.)

soaked in urine

I was waiting.
Holding a fifth of Vodka,
Bar-B-Q chips,
and two six packs of yeasty barley,
a man creeps behind me
headed for the cashier
(only his blue eyes exposed).
He holds something shiny
something black
aimed at the cashier in the
liquor store.

My heart racing
I pave way for the masked man
The cashier ducks.
SCREAMS!

"No please! Don't shoot, please don't shoot!"

What a coward!
Grab your gun and put one right between the eyes
He is a product of Hitler!

The cashier blew a hole in his chest
(the size of a softball)
The alleged "gunman" drops the flashlight

And it rolled and rolled and rolled
until it hit my
Black Doc Marten
standing on the red floor.

The cashier holds the smoking gun.
The malaise on the floor,
waiting to trudge his way to the pearly gates
with fingers crossed.

And when the woman
wearing a long black veil
entered the store
making the little silver bell sing,
she looked down at her body
(only her golden browns exposed;
shadowed by the longest eyelashes I have ever seen).

And it wasn't long until her head
leaned slightly to the left
(staring at the cashier).
Her right arm swung
from behind her back
and pointed
the pistol at his stupid face;
then gladly pulled the trigger
(smiling from her golden browns).

And by now
I am lying on the floor, thinking of her
Soaked in urine
Soaked in tears.

Milly the millner

"About 3 a.m. your hat will be ready to
mount your fiery head"

The blonde left downtown
and Milly's place
made of glass
furious with Milly
and her giant tits
and returned to her
Pink Cadillac
and bottle of
Scotch.

Meanwhile,
Milly sat in her red chair
until the wine manifested on her
tongue.

"Every time the red pot sings there are your words
Insurmountable jargon!
Aspirations of a prosperous life
My tits!"

The blonde returned
smothered in the
cold stench of a man's

Mercedes
13 smokes
3 pills
2 balls
1 shaft
and red and black
checkered coat
draped on her body.

"Here is your hat. I hope you like it."

And as her white head rolled on Milly's
dirty floor
she thought of the
crime she just committed.
So, Milly grabbed the woman's
Scotch
no ice
no glass
and another day of
screaming nightmares.

Later that year
Milly left the world with
one-fifth
32 smokes
and an empty room
shadowed by the
house next door

which was painted a heinous green.

the one they called Geo

Her name was Cassie
Blonde hair
blue eyes
vigorous body.

She lived on the corner of
Cherry Avenue and Broadway
in an old apartment that overlooked
the dirty water
the people in the park.

Every morning
they walked along the shore
waiting for the sun
their foggy breath floating
amid their pallid faces
waves washed their
yellow bruised feet
and her waning painted nails.

The morning ritual.

Every peaceful moon
she slept with her strange man;
the young man
with the gun

dark skin
straightened hair.

The one they call Geo.

One night
we rented a room for two
Seventh and Redondo;
a dirty room just for two with a broken lamp
a green blanket made from hemp
and a colored TV

And last Friday we drove,
up the coast and up the hill
to my ice-cold room.

It was dark and cold
covered with eyes.

Her smile left the room yesterday
and went to bed with

The One They Call geo.

red stain

... and when the doctor arrived
her ashen skin had changed to blue.

"here we go again!" said I

"I told her to wait her turn!" said he

And she drifted off into the interminable
sleep I filled the gun with
crystals and stabbed her.

Under the pages a red river
rolled on
to my waning soles.

So I gently kissed her lips
and made love
to her soon to be corpse.

(I felt her breathe, our lips finally touched)

"what happened?" "you died!" "died?"
"Died! and we made love while you slept"
"And it was perfect?" "died"

We drove to another part of town
another part of life
and did it all again.

the green hat

There was an old man and his mandolin
every night he played
on the dirty corner
of a dirty street
When people walked by
they put money in his old green hat
they walked away mumbling and cursing under their cloudy teeth
He was old and asleep
always wearing a black suit
while playing
his mandolin.
He played every night
of every week
of every month
of every year.
And when he played
they put money in his old green hat
then walked away with a grin of poise.
Every night at 3 a.m.
he walked alone
in the dark and up the hill
and emptied the green hat into strangers' hands.
Then every night
he closed his eyes
and dreamed of a faceless witch.

the color of sex and veneration

What a man!
an auspicious face
a straggly
gray
beard
a poet
a scholar
drives a '59
just like the one Elvis
squeezed into
and when he speaks
his eyes
are adorned by his mind.
If I were undaunted
in apprising
him of this,
I would
and if I were gay I would ask
him to dance ... but I'm not.

And what a woman!
her teeth
perfect.
Her grin holds an
embedded
sheen

like an old TV with
three channels and a
twisted
metal
hanger mounted on top.
Her skin
a starless
night.
Her decorum never wanes
not even once
a month
and if my
pale essence
was smirched
and
made brown
I would ask her name and
possibly tell her mine
But unfortunately ... it is not.

song of a junkie

You can't see what is inside
the plastic hollow tube
pasted with fading numbers at the mercy of a
junkie's touch.
Dirty water filtered through a piece of ripped
cotton?
One that will cease to cleanse
the inside of your skull?
Or tainted drops of
septic blood slivering through the silver
passage more than once and regifted to yours truly.
A wayfarer with stumps for
feet.
A rebellion quite analogous to God's plan.
So I sit drenched in flowers and jewels
waiting for it to piss black and white
a visage smothered in a deprecating grin
as the silver is ostracized from all that still
glistens.

the path

And every day
I stand by the same creek
on the same path
by the same school
and the same students walk by

some young some old

some vagabonds
wishing they would have listened to
their mothers and learned a thing or two
(If not for themselves that at least
for humanity.)

And the day is stretching!
Now the loitering sun
floats a little longer, before the
smile or pearl
is mounted in the night,
the same color as the neighbor's cat.

And every day
I stand there
watching them come
watching them go.

Crotches turning to asses
some smile
some snarl.

But all of them pass.
All of them leave
and that is what brings me back
to the same spot
by the same creek.

Day after sunny day.

a Sunday drive

Our drive was gilded.
The shadow of the islands
remind us of the balding
Hippy,
His jesters
His many books and
articles.

"Were going to be late" I told *her*
(Yes, the *child* with the
Golden Hair
who spends her days
eluding cretins and
smiling at anyone else she sees)
All she could do was laugh
and tell me,

"It's ok."

Now we sit in a
House of God
awaiting this perilous city
and all of its creatures
that crawl through the
night.

While the children play
and the preacher shouts.
We waited on our Sunday drive home.

A drive well worth it
just like Him
Just like *Her.*

thank God for mental illness

The homeless man babbles
rolls around on his wheelchair
spun out on countless cups of coffee
(probably speed as well).
A football player
San Marcos High School
Scholarships offered in the '70s.
Used to own four bars in
Santa Maria.

"I used to start drinking at noon," he says
Now we're getting somewhere.
Veracity!

The rain pours down,
flooding the entrance to the coffee shop,
us strangers try to do homework
babbling continues.

He's on to Captain Kirk,
(The name of the new bar he's going to open.)

The young Jewish woman looks up a number
so he can track down
an old friend
("there is no way I am going to pay two bucks to call 411!")

so he can chat about
his day.
Classy new bar.
Nameless new friends.

The talking evolves ...
It is apparent his brain is wet
from all the booze
from all the years.
He speaks with
intelligence
fast and alert with a significant
amount of
irreverence;
(at least to us students).
The rain continues.

The wheelchair is
spun
by the
wet-brained
owner
of the bar named after
The Captain
of the show the stoners
watch while eating
Chinese food.

(This is the time the police show up
for their free cup of coffee
and always take a second glance
at me once they notice
my attire,
but ultimately leave me alone

for a change
But I have a funny feeling they will take more than a second
glance at our wet-brained football star.)

William Shatner would be honored I am sure.

Thank God for Mental Illness.

babysitting the piano with a mouthful of gin

I told my sister I would watch
the girls
so they could drink
somewhere else;
leave the pile,
stagger the salted streets
until they vomit.
I played the piano all night,
my glass rarely empty,
a whole fist full of gin after
every song
until the bottle was hollowed
out
like a gutted fish.
I pounded on the
vulnerable keys of my
grandmother's
present she left me after
her soul had
had enough.
I played Charles
Manzarek
Cramps
The Damned.

Slurring the words of other
dead punks while the girls
played in the other room.
Midnight
1 o'clock
2 o'clock
I pounded away.
The girls shopped,
scribbled lipstick on their little
faces,
singing along to the songs
they knew from down the hall.
The smoke from a pack of
cigarettes crawled through
the air,
out the front door where the
fan was aimed.
Hopefully straight into the
neighbor's window;
(put them out of their misery)
I found three beers in the
interim,
drank them down, then
played some more.
The third beer was the night
capper,
or should I say morning.
I rested my head on the tired
keys;
one last demented chord,
as the sun crawled slowly up
the gray morning sky.

the morning paper by me

I wake up at 5 a.m. and turn on the TV
to the black-and-white channel; the only
channel without
those arbitrary commercials about buying
insurance from a woman named Flo.

I turn on the black-and-white channel
and watch Bette Davis and her gargantuan eyes.
I watch Fay Wray scream.
Brando mumble.

(Karl Malden's nose is something to remember too.)

Someone always plays the piano in these old movies:
unplugged and louder than anything
they've ever seen and I see the same house
the Western locales
over and over again,
adorned differently each time,
trying to make it seem like a whole new world.
While Billy Wilder yells "rolling!"
or when Hitchcock makes his habitual cameo.
They just don't make movies like the ones
I watch at 5 a.m. on the black-and-white channel.

The only channel without those
arbitrary commercials about buying insurance
from a woman named Flo.

the serpent in the village

There was a serpent and a village growing vast.
Rain dripped from the placid black sky.
The shadow of the trees hovered
amid the darkened village turning every day into night.
Oh such a beautiful night.

He slid through the village
on his shiny green blackish skin
peering at the children
roaming behind his emerald green eyes.
Following Samara to her quiet home
on the edge of town
every night when the moon was out
and the sun had left the sky.

"I've been watching you little girl
through my emerald eyes.
Your hair is black just like a princess in a fairy tale you see,
your lips are painted like the devil's dress
when drinking tea.
I've been watching you through my emerald eyes, you see."

And every day she walked by without a single
word from her lips.
Gaping at the crescent that teetered
amid the countless gems

he talked and hissed and blew her a kiss but never
caught her eye
her baby browns sparkled
sparkled like treasures in the sky.

Many years passed
many suns
many more moons
the serpent still slid through the village
on his scaly old skin.
Hissing at the aging woman
her shiny silver hair wrapped in black.
She wore the same red dress every day
as beautiful as the drunken sea.

Samara never wed in this desolate town.
She was growing old
her virgin skin was wrinkled
shrinking around her withered bones.
Yet she walked with sureness of her contemptuous solitary life
alone every day
alone in the uncanny purple night.

"I've been watching you, you see
through my emerald eyes
you have never loved a single man
never kissed his lips
but have danced alone on starry nights,
nights just like this,
I've been watching you, my dear
and you never gave a kiss."

She knew this was true
like the stories her father had told her;

two lovers poisoned
by the venom of their feeble
broken hearts.

"They danced with the devil
hand 'n hand at Central Park."

She told the serpent finally one night
when walking after dark.

"Don't be afraid dear
love can be tragic
beautiful you see
a black-winged dove
flying the uncanny purple sky
soaring high like an angel
among all the diamonds in the night
hastily dripping salty tears from its seductive
glistening eyes."

Samara listened to the serpent
its purple tongue crawled in and out—
—the clouds were moving in
smothering all the treasures in the night.
It started to rain.
Green raindrops landed on Samara's red dress
so she followed the serpent to his hollow cave
quick and out of sight.

(the walls were painted black and scarlet red
it was cold
the flame of the candle bounced about the
desolate hole)

In the middle of the room sat a wooden toy doll
inside a circle of rocks
there was no door; it was deep enough to turn black;
deep enough to turn cold.

She stared at the doll lying on its wooden back.
Asleep
The doll's face had tiny black eyes.
Its coat was painted green.
She picked up the doll, heard a man's voice, the loudest scream
(Samara bit her own lip until red dripped
and wished it was a dream).
"What is wrong my dear?
Why are your eyes filled with malevolent fear?
Why has your face been painted pastel shade soaked in salty tears?"

The serpent gave the doll a kiss on its dead face
looked at her through his emerald eyes
while she turned and ran away.

She ran through the dark
back to the village
to her isolated father hopping over
drunken bodies
lying inertly on the dirty floor.
When she reached her house she saw a conversant
face in the dark clouds
threw her black boots in the air
and busted down the red door

and there he hung still
he was not pendulous and his eyes gaped at her
a fire was burning below him
cracking like human bones hastily dying.

She fell to her knees and cried and mascara stained her
frail pallid hands.

"Daddy, Daddy I am scared and frightened.
that is why I am crying."

She told him, about the serpent
and his black and scarlet hole in the woods
about the wooden doll that slept on the floor
how the serpent and he kissed.
She wept as she spoke to him and tarnished the black
on her crumpled skin
and told her that they never kissed—that the serpent just slithered
and hissed.

Daddy stared with painted eyes
didn't speak a single word
so she walked up to him and gave him a gentle kiss
on his enclosed face
then she walked off to bed a dream of snakes
crawling through her skin
then she locked the door immortally
and never walked alone. Never again.

my obituary by Jon Vreeland

Jon Vreeland, America's most eminent writer since Ernest Hemingway and winner of the PEN/Faulkner award and the Nobel Prize, died of natural causes at his California Ranch last night. He was 100.

It was Dr. Emmet Brown who oversaw the autopsy and indicated Mr. Vreeland was in perfect health; it was just his lifelong patient's time to pass. "At 100 years old I think it's safe to say that Mr. Vreeland lived a long, full life. He outdid Elvis Presley by forty-eight years," says Brown.

Vreeland wrote over thirty books after he kicked his heroin addiction at age thirty-four. His first book, a memoir published by Vine Leaves Press, *The Taste of Cigarettes,* is the book that got his foot in the door. But it was his second novel, *Pretty Boys Wear Black* that put him on the map, often called the 21st century *Naked Lunch.* His novels and their graphic depictions have raised conflict with American figures and parents, calling the book "trash and bad for our children," says President Donald Trump, who is serving time in San Quentin Correctional Facility for conspiracy to murder.

Vreeland in many interviews explained the graphic nature of his novels and short stories and essays and claimed his goal was to scare and repulse people out of using lethal drugs, like heroin and methamphetamines. Take the rock-star fantasy from these amateur musicians who think that heroin and drugs make you a better member of the art community, and is needed for creative orgasm.

"Heroin is not a 'rockstar' thing to do. If accidentally using a bag of vomit for a pillow, or spilling a cup full of piss and laying in it [because that is the filth you are living in] sounds enticing and is 'rockstar,' then go right ahead, be my guest. Heroin and meth and drugs like those are your definite path to that kind of life," said Vreeland in a 2020 interview with Charlie Rose. Vreeland's novel, *And Then There Were Felines* shows the behavior in family's stifled by addiction, and was made into a major motion picture two years after the book's release in 2050. It also won the Pulitzer Prize that year.

Vreeland was born in Long Beach California. He was raised in Huntington Beach California. and raised two daughters, one who directed, *And Then There Were Felines,* Scarlett Rose. Vreeland struggled with addiction starting at the age of fifteen, and it haunted him until thirty-four, when he stole a car and ended up in a Santa Barbara jail, whose system helped him get into a drug treatment program and back to college where his writing career would begin.

By the time he finished college he would have his first two books published, granting him a job as the first ever Writer in Residence at Santa Barbara City College. He did this with no degree.

Vreeland, like most writers, kept very strange hours, often writing all through the night when the world was tired, sleeping only a few hours during the day. His ten acre ranch in Santa Barbara County was where he wrote ninety percent of his books, and lived fifty-four years with his wife who died ten years ago at age 100 as well. Her art is as famous as his books and their legacy lives on through their three children. Daughter's Mayzee Holland, eighty-two, Scarlett Rose, seventy-four, and son composer Preston Towers, eighty-three.

All three of his children were visiting Vreeland on the day of his death. He died peacefully in his sleep.

Jon Michael Vreeland
Vivid Man, Vibrant Soul

Ask people to describe Jon Michael Vreeland, and the response is an outpouring of praise and adulation. The word "talented" plays on repeat. Other accolades include brilliant, intelligent, witty, beautiful, kind, and thoughtful. Among the many messages of love and grief that Jon's family, friends, and fans wrote on the Tribute Wall created after his death, were these: "Jon meant well to everyone." "The world is a colder place without him."

Another adjective that describes Jon is "vivid," defined as "producing intense feelings or mental images." Everything about Jon's presence was intense and provoked an equal reaction from others. He was also "vibrant," that is, "full of energy and enthusiasm." The force that was Jon is so potent that its power lives on long after him. He was a man of strong emotions. These included anger (Jon had a temper); fear (normally brave, he was nevertheless scared of spiders and sharks); and odd dislikes (he was bothered by smells such as lavender and cologne).

Yet Jon was more often filled with passion for the good things that "rocked his world," and was driven to share his enthusiasms with others. He loved yoga and wanted to teach its asanas and benefits to everyone. A look at a few of Jon's other loves reveals his quirkiness and charm. Take food. He couldn't boil water but loved everything Alycia cooked for him. Italian dishes were his favorite. So was Sour Patch Extreme Sour Flavor Candy, which he discovered after smoking weed out of an apple. Jon preferred English black tea over coffee, an unusual and independent choice for a man whose literary idols thrived in an era of burgeoning coffee houses. Old movies were also high on Jon's love list, especially black-and-white classics like Marlon Brando's 1951 film *A Street Car Named Desire.* He adored Betty Davis, crushed on Olivia deHavilland, and was obsessed with Harry Carey Jr., famous for his roles in John Ford Westerns. Jon was thrilled to receive one of the actor's ascots from his "badass" friend Melinda Carey.

Musically, Jon could never get enough of Iron Butterfly's *In a gadda da vida. Grapefruit Moon* was one of his favorite Tom Waits' songs. *Big Cats* was his number one television show. It's easy to see why. The beauty, grace, and ferocity of these awesome creatures evoke a vision of Jon prowling the world for inspiration. Inspiration was his prey. When Alycia's best friend did a photo shoot and asked Jon how he wanted people to see him, Jon replied, "I want people to know I am unique." This vivid and vibrant man most certainly was! Read on to remember, savor, and treasure how Jon presented himself to the world and touched so many lives.

A Talented Man

Blessed with a multitude of talents, Jon wore many hats including craftsman, musician, writer, teacher, even baseball player. For starters, he was a skilled woodworker, whether helping his father or striking out on his own. Jon's specialties were crown molding, ornate fireplace mantles, and hardwood flooring. His artistry is evident in the finely executed work he left behind.

A Musician

Jon's talents as a musician are legendary. He was a gifted and classically trained pianist who was also a professional keyboard player for the band Citizen, and a keyboard-organist for the Huntington Beach punk band Stink Eye. His friend and fellow musician Selden Cummings said, "Jon is one of those pianists with 'the gift' who can sit down at the bench and make magic with his fingers, seemingly without even thinking about it." Jon's style was emulated by admirers who aspired to play with his skill and fearsomeness. On his Tribute Wall, one of the many people he encouraged wrote, "I have a love for the piano and Jon swore he could teach me to play as well as he could. LOL. I'll take what you taught me and work at it." In addition to playing and teaching others, Jon was also a music producer, who translated his auditory images into sounds that others could hear and respond to, recording and promoting his musician friends.

A Writer

A multi-genre author, Jon was fascinated by literature. He researched the subject in the belief that reading made you a better writer. In Jon's case, studying enhanced his innate talent. He reached a worldwide audience with *The Taste of Cigarettes: A Memoir of a Heroin Addict,* which was published by Vine Leaves Press in 2018. Drug addiction was often the muse for Jon's work. He liked to shock his readers in the hope of scaring them straight. Peter Snell, a former bookstore owner who later became Jon's good friend, reviewed the manuscript for VLP. He says "It was so powerful and so engagingly written that I was hooked" and he recommended the memoir for publication. His faith was borne out. It continues to be on of VLP's best-sellers.

Jon was also a journalist. He freelanced for the *Montecito Journal,* the *Santa Barbara Sentinel,* and despite his own liberal values, even the relatively conservative *Santa Barbara News Press,* where he wrote profiles on singular characters in his own inimitable voice. He honed his formidable talents as a creative writing student at Santa Barbara City College (SBCC), where faculty members commented, "We helped polish the skills he already had." He was president of the SBCC Creative Writing Club and wrote for *The Channels,* the campus newspaper. In 2016, Jon was awarded the William Olivarius scholarship, given annually to an outstanding English major. He was so proud, as was his family. Everyone had faith in Jon.

As a writer, Jon worshiped three demi-gods. He was inspired by the brazen honesty and unabashed vulgarity of Charles Bukowski; fancied himself the reincarnation of Ernest Hemingway; and emulated Hunter S. Thompson's gonzo journalistic style. Like his heroes, Jon didn't shy away from tough topics, including addiction and racism. SBCC has a video of students listening with rapt attention as Jon reads a story about white privilege. In addition to being a memoirist and journalist, Jon was also a playwright and essayist. Above all, however, Jon wanted to be known as a poet. Says his wife Alycia, "So he wore his little cap, had his little cigarette thing, and a copy of *Howl* in his pocket, and spoke with anybody who wanted to talk about poetry." It's an affectionate and wistful image of a man who was exactly what he aspired to be.

Before Jon's death, he was working on two books. *A Church Named Sally* is about his experience with The Salvation Army and *Pretty Boys Wear Black* is a continuation of his memoir, revolving around Jon's jail time. Alycia hopes to publish the manuscripts posthumously with royalties going to his children, as Jon would have wished. Says his friend, Peter Snell, "Jon had a voice and a way with words. As long as his words are alive, then surely so too is his spirit."

A Mentor

Jon held miscellaneous jobs as a construction worker, gas station attendant, hotel bellhop, and employee at Dave's Waves Christmas Tree Lots, where he earned holiday money. But with his talent for generosity, he was always a mentor and teacher. Says Alycia, "When he'd meet somebody he'd go 'What's your thing, something that makes you cool, different, or unique?' Jon just wanted people to find their 'thing' and let it fly." He did this as an English tutor at SBCC, in fact, with anyone who stepped inside his creative circle. Says his erstwhile classmate and fellow writer Selden Cummings, "More than anyone I know, Jon wants to make those around him believe in achieving their wildest dreams." Jon led the way for so many people.

Perhaps most memorable is the encouragement he gave Alycia that let her "fly" as an artist. She'd only worked in watercolor before meeting Jon. Challenging her to engage with a more challenging medium, he bought her a canvas, her first, spurring her to paint in acrylics. Her muse was Frida Kahlo until one day Jon said, "You're so amazing. Why don't you do a character based on yourself?" And that's how Baby Darlin'—Alycia's signature image—was born. Even now, she feels his presence when she works: "Jon is my creative angel and looks out for me."

A Son

Jon and his dad, Jon Gordon Vreeland, were very close. The father, like the son, performed many roles. He was a fireman, ran a video game rental business, and owned the woodworking business where Jon learned the craft. His dad supported Jon by throwing baseballs with him for practice and paying for piano lessons. He recalls that Jon used to watch *The Music Man* over and over as a child and astutely observed, "Of course the film was about books and music. It obviously had a huge effect on him." At the same time he encouraged his son, Jon's dad could be authoritarian and was hard on him.

Through it all, Jon's dad maintained a heart of gold and tried to rescue Jon from the streets many times, to no avail. Still, he continued to visit, bringing food, and let Jon know he was loved. Jon wanted so much to be like his father, the family breadwinner. He strove to impress the man he looked up to, but never felt he was good enough. His father urged him to go to college and get a steady job, accomplishments that eluded Jon for many years. Finally, when Jon became a published author, he felt that he'd met his father's expectations and gained his acceptance. On the day of Jon's book launch at Chaucer's Bookstore in Santa Barbara, with his father and the rest of the family looking on proudly, Jon excitedly told his friend and fellow writer Selden Cummings, "It's like I'm finally a real writer. I'm on the shelves. People will come in here and they'll be looking through stuff and they'll see Bukowski, and Kafka, and *Vreeland.*"

Jon's mother, Alyson Vreeland, worked at the high school with special needs children. Jon was especially close to her, a "mama's boy" and not ashamed to admit it. In his eyes, his mother could do no wrong. Her son could call and talk to her about everything. Alyson loved Jon and his sister Christa back, but she also had firm rules for her children. She tried hard to get her son into treatment several times. Like Jon's father, his mother was at a loss about what to do.

When addiction invades a family, the puzzling dilemma, "What can we do?" lives beside the nagging question, "Why did it happen?" In many ways, the Vreelands fit the picture of a wholesome American family. They went boating, took long drives, and enjoyed camping trips in their van. There were huge dinners and holiday gatherings with the extended family, plates piled high with delicious food. Jon's parents tried valiantly to keep their son in sober living. It was hard on them to watch him struggle. When Jon moved to Santa Barbara and met Alycia, they were so excited that he was finally away from the drugs and the toxic environment that held him in their grip. At last, Jon was in school and holding down a job. Above all, their boy was happy.

A Father

Jon doted on his daughters, Mayzee and Scarlett. The girls were the most important people in his life; he would do anything for them. Unlike many parents, he was non-judgmental. Jon accepted and adored them for who they were, regardless. Seeing them at Jon's book launch, Selden Cummings described them as "uncannily attractive ... like actresses who wandered off a movie set and into the store." Evoking the image in the iconic sunscreen ad, Jon called them his "Coppertone girls." He loved them but they were often told their father was too sick to see them. Visits were only allowed when Jon was sober.

Nevertheless, Jon and his older daughter Mayzee were very close. Because Jon was so young when she was born, they essentially grew up together. He was so proud that he was the one who bought Mayzee her first car, and he was teaching her to play the piano. Jon called her every day. Like her father, Mayzee struggles with addiction. Yet she's grown into a lovely young woman with all of her dad's best qualities.

Jon was also very proud of his daughter Scarlett. She was his baby. He taught her how to fish on the Santa Barbara pier and loved watching her dance at ballet recitals. Jon didn't hesitate to tell others about Scarlett's grace, beauty, and intelligence either. He posted photos of his baby on social media, inviting everyone to admire her as much as he did.

Jon regarded his daughters as his best creations. He desperately wanted to be the kind of father who was there for them, emotionally and physically, and was hard on himself when he couldn't meet his own expectations for that role. However, when he was with them, Jon was fully present. When Jon and Alycia visited them in Huntington Beach, the girls loved going to lunch and shopping for records with them. Jon was so proud to have the money to buy their back-to-school clothes at Fashion Island in Newport Beach. Although this life review was not written *by* them, they are among the primary readers it was written *for*. Jon is looking after and over his daughters, gifting Mayzee and Scarlett with his irrepressible energy and unlimited love.

A Husband

Jon's two early intimate relationships, including one marriage, ended due to his addiction. The lasting benefit from each was a daughter. True love came when Jon moved to Santa Barbara and met Alycia. They married in 2014. Because they both faced the demon of addiction, they could understand and support each other during recovery. It was actually Jon's daughters who brought them together. Says Alycia: "I met Jon through the love of his girls. I happened to be sneaking a peek over his shoulder at a church meeting as he was admiring photographs of them on his phone. I commented on how beautiful they were. He turned around with a great big smile of pride and joy and informed me that they were his precious daughters." Two loves led to a third.

If that beginning was ordained, the circumstances of their first date were less predictable. Alycia describes it this way: "Jon invited me to a 'skate date' because he saw a skateboard in one of my Facebook pictures. I had to build up the courage to confess that I hadn't stepped on a skateboard for nearly twenty years." However, when she saw how patient and kind Jon was re-teaching her, he won her heart. Below are some of the memories she cherishes from their years together. Random as they initially seem, they cohere into a portrait of a magical marriage.

The crows wake us up every morning. I get annoyed by the loud cawing chatter. Jon gets excited and finds some bread or crackers to feed them, talks to them as if they are friends. And now we have a murder of crows that visit our front door every morning.

This happened often. "Hurry get off the couch, come outside look at the moon, isn't it magnificent, witchy amazing?" he yells, dragging me to my feet. We both start howling at the moon, laughing and dancing around.

Full moon cemetery walks became a ritual. Jon felt compelled to talk to the grieving people bent over their loved one's graves. He had such a compassionate heart.

Fun things: Watching old movies; grooving to favorite music; dressing up; letting me butcher his hair many times; he loved to have his head scratched.

Serious things: Talking about our Special Purpose, spirituality, Catholicism; our song is *God Only Knows* by the Beach Boys.

Jon wanted to grow old with me on a farm and have his three children live in homes on site.

Jon had an inquisitive mind and artistic intelligence. He was smart and passionate in ways that matched mine. We had chemistry and physical attraction. I'll love him 'til the end of time. Jon is my creative angel looking out for me. I feel this ... I really feel this.

Alycia's memories, like those of Jon's parents and daughters, friends and colleagues, are indelible. Death doesn't erase them. Jon's absence only makes them more vivid.

A Forever Man

A friend wrote on Jon's Tribute Wall: "Life is not always easy on the gentle and kind." For all of his gifts, and all the love he received and gave to others, Jon battled demons, most notably heroin addiction. "It's called 'chasing the dragon.' For some college students it is the deadliest pastime since Russian Roulette," he wrote in his first staff column for *The Channels* in 2016, a glimpse into his writing style where he invited readers to share his darkest moments. His honesty took courage; his warnings came from a place of experience and care.

He paid the consequences. Jon served time and was embarrassed by his jailhouse tattoos—wings on his back. But he was beginning to confront his incarceration in the continuation of his memoir, *Pretty Boys Wear Black,* and hoped to turn personal adversity into inspiration for others. Here is Alycia's take on those wings: "I believe they're getting proper use now. I think he will be proud. Jon thought if he died, no one would care. We proved him wrong. He is so loved and remembered. Use those wings and please help us out down here, hip cowboy poet angel."

Jon Michael Vreeland was born in Huntington Beach, California, on July 13, 1979. He died in Santa Barbara, California on September 15, 2020, age forty-one, waiting for a bed to open in rehab. His body was filled with heroin and meth, but the exact circumstances of his death remain unclear. He was living in a homeless encampment near Mission Creek, on a grassy ledge beneath a footbridge above the creek, and fell into a concrete drainage culvert, twenty feet below. The fall may have been the result of an accident, or an overdose. Some say that he'd gotten into a fight and was pushed, but possible informants are not talking or are themselves dead.

For those who knew and loved Jon, the ambiguity of his death adds to the pain of their loss. What is not ambiguous, however, is that Jon was a colorful, creative, and compassionate force who lives on through the indelible words and memories he left behind.

"Death has eyes of ruby mirrors, skin of sapphire junk." J.V., poet

Contributors

Alycia Vreeland (Jon's wife)
Jon Gordon Vreeland (Jon's father)
Selden Cummings (Jon's friend)
Peter Snell (Jon's friend)

Compiled by Ann S. Epstein
Writer and End-of-Life Doula

Acknowledgements

I express heartfelt gratitude to Jon for his idea of designing this book and always supporting my creativity. We started the book in 2015 and sadly after Jon left us for spiritland, I transposed his writing and completed the last few illustrations in his memory. He would be pleased to know he is a published poet.

I want to thank everyone at Vine Leaves Press. Jessica Bell, Amie McCracken, Melanie Faith. Peter Snell for humor and encouragement, Ann S. Epstein, Chella Courington for encouraging Jon to find his voice, Chelsea Lancaster for always reading Jon's work J. Grisham and S. Snowbarger.

Selden Cummings, Kirk Shaffer and all of his readers.

Tim Buckley for believing in Jon's Gonzo style journalism at *The Montecito Journal.*

The Sentinel, Rebelle Society, East Fork, Sun and Sandstone, Plain Brown Wrapper, and *Painted Cave.*

Thank you to everyone who supports my art. Didi Sterling inspiring new characters. Thank you Emmanuel Itier and Wonderland Entertainment for including my art in *The Cure, Guns, Bombs, and War: A Love Story, Tuck Magazine, Rebel Society, Painted Cave* and *The Montecito Journal.*

Thank you to my Rhodes and Vreeland Family for your love and support. Thank you Preston for continuing on with our family's creative gift. Mayzee and Scarlett for always supporting their dad's writing. Thank you to my tribe.

I am grateful to walk in God's grace with a tribe who supports me no matter what.

www.ingramcontent.com/pod-product-compliance
Ingram Content Group UK Ltd.
Pitfield, Milton Keynes, MK11 3LW, UK
UKHW041639190726
13854UKWH00006B/2587

9 783988 320797